A gift for

_____

From

Tiny Tidings of Joy

for You, Friend

Illustrations by Amy Rosenberg

COUNTRYMAN

Babbling Brook
Little Works of Heart

Published by J. Countryman, a division of
Thomas Nelson, Inc., Nashville, Tennessee 37214

Project Editor: Terri Gibbs

Designed by Left Coast Design Inc., Portland, Oregon

ISBN: 08499-9666-X

www.jcountryman.com

Printed in USA

A tiny tiding
of good cheer
just for you—
a friend so dear!

Friends are
like gifts—
whether
large or
small
we treasure
them all.

Though it may snow
and cold winds blow,

we'll warm our hearts with
Christmas cheer,

and think of friends
both far and near.

If I could give you any gift in the world, I'd give you:

_____

_____

_____

_____

_____

_____

_____

_____

_____

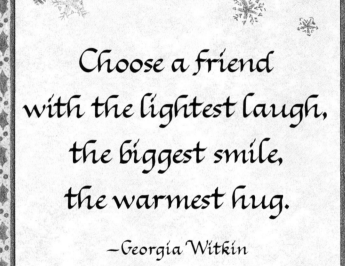

Choose a friend
with the lightest laugh,
the biggest smile,
the warmest hug.

–Georgia Witkin

One can never be too good to a friend.

When does
Christmas start?
With greenery and
ribbon bows,
and gently falling snow?
Or when simple things
like love and joy
start tugging
at your heart.

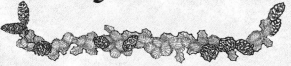

Here are some of the things
I find delightful about you:

_____

_____

_____

_____

_____

_____

_____

_____

_____

Blessed be the LORD your God

who has delighted in you. 1 Kings 10:9

Christmas is
the time of year...

that's touched
with angel wings.

Let's celebrate
the Christ child's birth,
God come down
from heaven to earth.
Look above
where bright stars shine,
rejoice, be glad,
it's Christmastime!

A little Christmas prayer for you:

_____

_____

_____

_____

_____

_____

_____

_____

One can never have too many friends

. . . or Christmas cookies!

Christmas
is coming!
What shall we do?
We'll fill the days
with memories,
to last the whole
year through.

My Christmas wish
for you will be:

"May you enjoy as
much gladness
as you've given to me!"